DATE DUE

LET'S INVESTIGATE SCIENCE
SCIENCE
The Weather

LET'S INVESTIGATE SCIENCE
The Weather

Robin Kerrod

Illustrated by Ted Evans

MARSHALL CAVENDISH
NEW YORK · LONDON · TORONTO · SYDNEY

Library Edition Published 1994

© Marshall Cavendish Corporation 1994

Published by Marshall Cavendish Corporation
2415 Jerusalem Avenue
PO Box 587
North Bellmore
New York 11710

Series created by Graham Beehag Book Design

Library of Congress Cataloging-in-Publication Data

Kerrod, Robin.
    The Weather / Robin Kerrod; llustrated by Ted Evans.
    p. cm. -- (Let's investigate science)
    Includes index.
    ISBN 1-85435-630-5   ISBN 1-85435-688-7 (set)
    1. Weather--Juvenile literature. 2. meteorology--Juvenile literature.
    [1. Weather. 2. Meteorology.] I. Evans, Ted ill.   II. Title.   III. Series: Kerrod,
Robin.
    Let's investigate science.
    QC981.3.K47 1994   93-49706
    551.5--dc20   CIP
                                                              AC

Printed and bound in Hong Kong.

Contents

Introduction

The weather is one of the most common topics of conversation throughout the world, and for good reason. The weather affects everyone in one way or another most of the time, determining what we wear, how we spend our leisure time, and so forth.

There are many pleasant aspects to the weather: sunny days to enjoy on the beach, cooling sea breezes, fresh snow for skiing, and strong winds for sailing. But there are also many unpleasant aspects, which can put people's jobs and lives at risk. These aspects include severe frosts, floods, droughts, storms, blizzards, hurricanes, and tornadoes. Such weather hazards ruin property and injure or kill thousands of people around the world every year.

This book describes the many different aspects of the weather and covers the scientific principles behind them. Following an expanded introductory section, the three chapters cover the main aspects that determine the weather – air and its movement, moisture in the air, and temperature and climate.

You can check your answers to the questions featured throughout this book on pages 60-61.

◄ **A spectacular sunset. An old country saying is that such a brilliant "red sky at night" is a "sailor's delight" and promises a fine day in the morning. In practice the chances of a fine day following a red sunset are even.**

Broadly speaking, we can describe weather as the condition of the air around us – hot or cold, wet or dry, still or windy, clear or cloudy, and so on. For the temperature to rise, or the winds to blow, energy must be put into the atmosphere. The main source of this energy is the Sun.

The Sun

Even though it is an average of some 93 million miles (150 million km) away, the Sun pours abundant energy on the Earth in the form of heat, light, and other radiation.

Of course, the Sun shines on only about half of the Earth at any moment. This is the part facing the Sun, where it is daytime. The other half of the Earth is in darkness, and it is nighttime.

During the night, the Earth loses much of the heat it received from the Sun during the day. This makes the temperature fall and helps set up movements in the atmosphere that bring about weather changes. Unequal heating of different regions of the Earth by the Sun also helps drive the world's weather systems.

▲ The Sun gives out a yellowish-white light, but at sunset it takes on a reddish hue. This is because dust in the lower part of the atmosphere blocks most of the wavelengths (colors) in light except red.

Q What is the main difference between these solar flames and the flame of a burning candle?

The atmosphere

It is the interaction of the Sun and the atmosphere that gives us our weather. The atmosphere is a layer of gases that covers our Earth to a thickness of about 500 miles (800 km).

The atmosphere is not the same density all the way up. It is densest closest to the ground, and gets progressively less dense the higher you go. At a height of about 500 miles (800 km), there is virtually no air left at all and the atmosphere merges into space.

▶▶ This diagram (which is not to scale) shows a beam of solar radiation hitting the Earth. Only about half of the energy in the beam reaches the Earth's surface: some is reflected back into space by the Earth's atmosphere; some is absorbed by the atmosphere; some is reflected and absorbed by clouds; and some is reflected by the ground. The remainder is absorbed by the Earth's surface, both land and water, and heats them up.

8

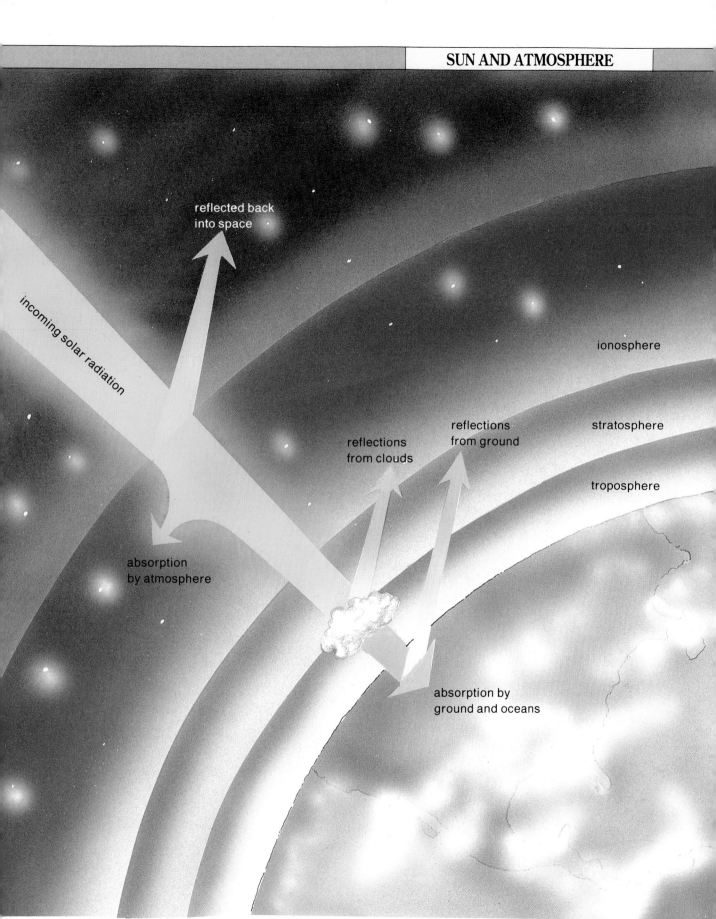

reflected back
into space

incoming solar radiation

ionosphere

reflections
from ground

reflections
from clouds

stratosphere

troposphere

absorption
by atmosphere

absorption by
ground and oceans

1.

The three main features that determine the weather at any place and at any time: the temperature of the air (1), air pressure and movement (2), and the amount of moisture in the air (3).

2.

countries. Weather has no boundaries, of course, so it is essential that meteorologists know what weather systems are approaching their own country from farther afield. The main source of weather data from around the world is the World Meteorological Organization (WMO). Member countries feed their own weather data into the WMO computer, which is them available for use by other members via high-speed communications links.

These days meteorologists can also access weather data directly from weather satellites, which circle the Earth at a distance of hundreds

Weather basics

The study of weather is called meteorology, and the scientists who study it are called meteorologists.

Their job involves measuring weather conditions at regular intervals through the day and night. They work at weather stations dotted around the country, using a variety of different instruments, such as barometers to measure air pressure and hygrometers to measure humidity.

Meteorologists also receive data on weather around the world from meteorologists in other

3.

or even thousands of miles. They give a truly global view of the Earth's weather systems, sending back pictures of clouds as well as measurements.

Weather forecasting

Armed with up-to-the-minute data on conditions in the atmosphere, meteorologists then try to predict how the weather is going to change in the short term and in the long term. These predictions form the weather forecasts we see in the newspapers and on television.

▼ **(Below) Several GOES satellites like this circle the Earth, sending back pictures of cloud cover.**

▼ **(Bottom) A NOAA satellite returned this picture as it flew over North America. The picture shows most of the U.S. clearly, but there are plenty of clouds to the east and southeast.**

Q **What are the dark areas near the top of the picture?**

11

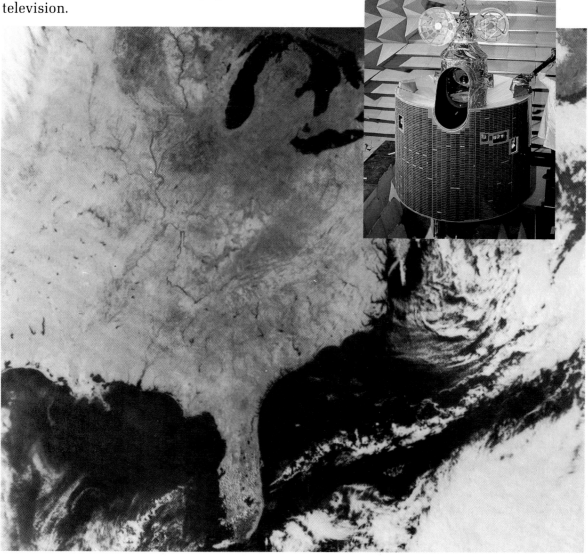

Weather maps

To help them make their weather forecasts, meteorologists draw up a series of weather maps. The first one they prepare is a synoptic chart, which presents a synopsis, or summary, of weather conditions at a certain time.

On the synoptic chart, meteorologists record the weather conditions reported at weather stations around the country and elsewhere at a certain time. These conditions include temperature, air pressure, wind speed and direction, and percipitation (rain, snow, and sleet).

After all the weather readings have been plotted, lines called isobars are drawn linking places with equal air pressure. Centers of high pressure ("highs") and low pressure ("lows") are also marked, as are the "fronts," or boundaries between different air masses.

By studying the newly prepared synopsis chart and other charts they prepared earlier, meteorologists can get a good idea of how the weather is changing. Armed with this information, they now draw up what is called a prognostic chart. This map shows the predicted weather conditions at a certain time in the future. It shows the predicted positions of isobars, "highs" and "lows," and fronts. Using the information on this chart, they are now ready to issue their weather forecast.

►► This is a kind of simplified weather map found in many newspapers. It shows in color code the predicted pattern of temperature over the United States on a day in November. The map also includes details of precipitation, such as rain and snow.

12

A series of weather maps, which show how the weather in the Noerthern Atlantic changes over a three-day period. They illustrate how a weather system, born off eastern North America, races eastward over the ocean and hits western Europe two days later.

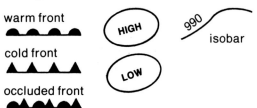

▲ Some of the features found on a weather map: isobars, centers of high and low air pressure, and weather fronts. They appear, for example, in the series of Atlantic weather maps.

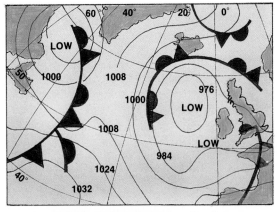

1. A weather front has developed in the western Atlantic. There is a center of low pressure in the north.

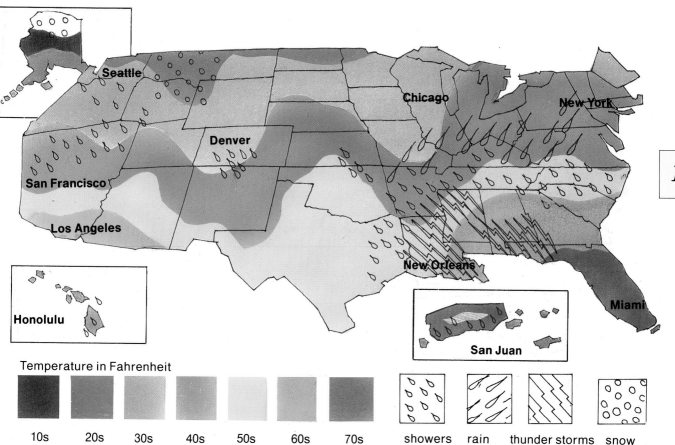

Temperature in Fahrenheit

10s   20s   30s   40s   50s   60s   70s   showers   rain   thunder storms   snow

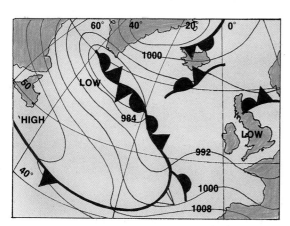

2. The "low" hasn't moved a lot, but the associated front has swept out into the mid-Atlantic.

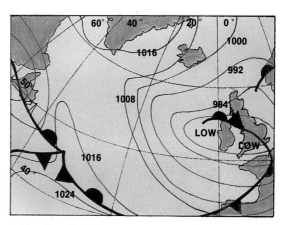

3. The "low" has raced across the ocean and developed into a severe depression over western Europe. Isobars are close together, indicating that winds will be strong to gale force.

Weather on other worlds

We are familiar with the weather on Earth, but what is the weather like on the other planets in our Solar System?

Both our closest neighbor in space – the Moon – and the planet closest to the Sun – Mercury – have little weather to speak of because they have no atmosphere. They are very hot during the day and very cold during the night.

The other planets do, however, have an atmosphere. But their atmospheres are quite different from that of the Earth. Perhaps the most interesting planets are our two neighbors, Venus and Mars. They are interesting because we may in the foreseeable future be able to visit them. So what is their weather like?

Venus has an atmosphere made up mainly of carbon dioxide, and its pressure is nearly 100 times that on Earth. And the temperature at the surface of Venus is hot enough to melt lead – over 850°F (455°C). We can't see the surface from Earth because it is permanently covered by thick white clouds of sulfuric acid droplets. Venus is not a very friendly place!

Mars also has an atmosphere of carbon dioxide, but only a very thin one. The temperature is much lower than it is on Earth, struggling above freezing only during the

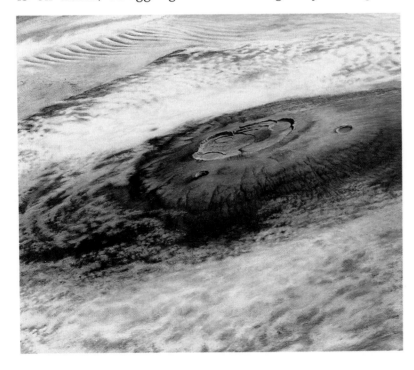

◄ Clouds gather around the slopes of the huge extinct volcano on Mars known as Olympus Mons (Mt. Olympus). They are clouds of ice crystals.

14

▲ Of all the moons in the Solar System, this one – Saturn's moon Titan – is the only one that has an atmosphere. The main gas in the atmosphere is nitrogen; there is also some methane. Scientists figure that the methane in Titan's atmosphere acts in the same way that water vapor acts in the Earth's atmosphere. They think that Titan's weather is misty and "damp" with methane, and when it rains, it rains methane.

Q 1. Nitrogen is also the main gas in the atmosphere of one of the nine planets in the Solar System. Which one?

Martian summer. Despite the low pressures and temperatures, however, winds blow on Mars, and clouds of water ice form over the high ground. Ice caps also grow at the poles during the Martian winter.

Beyond Mars are the giant planets Jupiter, Saturn, Uranus, and Neptune, and the tiny outermost planet Pluto. Pluto is made up of rock and frozen gas. But the giants are made up mainly of light gases, such as hydrogen and helium. They have very deep atmospheres, in which winds howl at speeds of many hundreds of miles an hour. Great storms occur in their atmospheres, like hurricanes on Earth but much bigger. Underneath the light gases there are great oceans of liquid gas. One can't even guess what the ocean weather is like.

15

◄ The bands in the atmosphere of Saturn show layers of clouds traveling at different speeds.

Q 2. The fastest clouds on Saturn travel at speeds of more than 1,600 feet (488 meters) per second. What is this speed in mph (km/h)?

► Colorful clouds and swirling gases race furiously around the most prominent feature on Jupiter – the Great Red Spot. This huge oval disturbance in the planet's atmosphere is the "eye" of a gigantic storm that has been raging for centuries.

Q 3. The Spot is about 17,500 miles (28,000 km) long and about 9,000 miles (14,000 km) across. If the circumference of the Earth is about 25,000 miles (40,000 km), how many Earths could you fit into the spot?

1 Air on the Move

◄ Clouds spiral around a center of low pressure in the north Atlantic Ocean. They are caused by battling masses of cold and warm air.

The atmosphere extends above the Earth to a height of several hundred miles. But our weather occurs in the lowest part of the atmosphere, in a region we call the troposphere. The troposphere varies in depth from about 6 miles (10 km) at the North and South Poles, to about 12 miles (20 km) at the Equator.

It is in the troposphere that clouds form, rain and snow fall, and winds blow. Winds are movements of the air. They can be gentle breezes, welcome on a hot summer's day, or furious hurricanes, which leave in their wake a trail of death and destruction. On a broader scale, great masses of air move around the world affecting the weather of continents.

Above the troposphere is a layer of rarefied air called the stratosphere, which extends up to about 50 miles (80 km). Above that, in the ionosphere, there is hardly any air left at all. Several hundred miles up, at the end of the ionosphere, the atmosphere gradually merges into space.

Q Can you think of any reason why the troposphere would be deeper near the Equator?

► The trunks of trees near the seashore are often bent like this. They are bent by strong breezes blowing continually off the sea.

The air around us

We owe not only our weather, but also our life on Earth to the atmosphere. The air that makes up the atmosphere contains the gas that we and all other living things must breathe to stay alive. This gas is oxygen. The Investigation will give you a rough idea of how much oxygen there is in the air.

The other main gas in the air is nitrogen. There are also traces of several other gases. One is hydrogen oxide or, to give it a more familiar name, water vapor. This gas is present only in tiny amounts, but it has a remarkable effect on the weather (see Chapter 3).

Among the other gases is carbon dioxide, which is the gas living things give off when they breathe out.

Q What else gives off carbon dioxide?

INVESTIGATE

Find out the rough proportion of oxygen in the air with this simple experiment. Stick a candle on the base of a bowl with a piece of modeling clay. Pour an inch or so of water into the bowl, then light the candle. Place a jar over the lighted candle. Be careful you don't put your hand in the candle flame.

In a few minutes, the candle will go out as it burns up the oxygen in the air in the jar. Notice that the water has risen inside the jar. With a crayon, mark where the water level inside the jar reaches.

Now figure out the proportion of oxygen in the air in the jar. How do you do this?

WORKOUT

Hold out one of your hands, palm upwards, and roughly calculate its area by measurement. Using the value for atmospheric pressure mentioned in the text, figure out what weight of air is pressing down on your palm.

If you lived in New York City, would the weight of air pressing on your palm be larger or smaller than if you lived in Denver, Colorado?

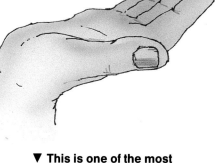

▼ This is one of the most common weather instruments, the barograph. It records how the air pressure changes with time as a tracing on paper. The paper is wrapped around a slowly moving drum. The bellows device is an evacuated, or airless, chamber, which rises or falls as the air pressure changes. This movement is transmitted to a pointer, which marks the paper.

Q 2. It would be simpler to attach the pointer to the bellows device without having the pivot mechanism. What is the drawback of this simpler design?

The warm blanket

Life on Earth would also be difficult without the blanketing effect of the atmosphere. The atmosphere acts like a greenhouse and traps much of the heat the Earth receives from the Sun. This helps keep us warm, particularly at night, by preventing too much heat from escaping back into space.

The atmosphere has yet another feature that favors life on Earth. High up in the stratosphere, there is a layer of a gas called ozone, which is a different kind of oxygen. This layer filters out of sunlight the harmful radiation, called ultraviolet rays.

Q 1. In summer, despite the ozone layer, ultraviolet rays are still strong enough to affect us. What do they do?

Atmospheric pressure

We are not aware of it, but the air in the atmosphere has weight. It presses down on us and everything else on the Earth's surface with a force of about 14.7 pounds on every square inch (1 kg on every square meter). This figure is called the atmospheric pressure.

The atmospheric pressure changes slightly from time to time and from place to place. These differences in pressure make the air move, carrying different weather from place to place. Meteorologists measure air pressure with a barometer or barograph (a recording barometer).

Falling air pressure is usually a bad sign, indicating that rain may be on the way. Rising air pressure, however, is usually a good sign, bringing with it the promise of fine, clear weather.

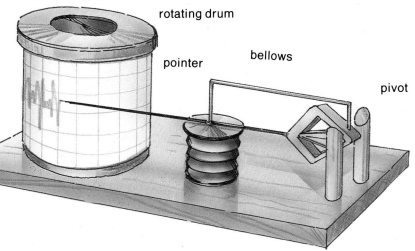

rotating drum

pointer

bellows

pivot

Winds and breezes

When air is heated, it rises. You can feel the hot air rising from a radiator in your home. The air rises because, when it is heated, it becomes lighter, or less dense, than the surrounding cool air.

This cool air now moves in above the radiator to take the place of the hot air that has risen. In turn, this cool air becomes hot and rises, and is replaced by more cool air. This process, which is called convection, causes the air in your home to circulate.

At the seaside, light breezes often spring up even when it is calm farther inland. These breezes occur mainly because of the different heat properties of land and water.

◄ During the day, the land heats up faster than the sea. This sets up a local circulation in the atmosphere, as shown in the diagram. A breeze blows inland from off the sea.

◄ During the night, the land cools down faster than the sea. This sets up a circulation in the atmosphere in the opposite direction from what it is during the day. A breeze blows from the land out to sea.

◄ A cup anemometer and a weather vane, mounted together at a small weather station to measure wind speed and direction. They are connected to instruments inside the station, which record their measurements automatically. Note in the sky the wisps of cirrus clouds, heralding an imminent change in the weather.

Similar processes are at work on the Earth's surface, which set the air in motion and create the winds. For example, on a summer's day at the shore, the hot land acts like the radiator just mentioned and causes the air to move, creating what we call a sea breeze.

We could also have explained the circulation of the air in terms of pressure differences. Where hot, light air is rising, it presses down less. When cold, heavy air is sinking, it presses down more. So where there are temperature differences over the Earth, there are also differences in pressure. The air then moves to equalize the pressure, creating the winds.

Wind force

We use the term "breeze" for a light-to-strong wind, up to a speed of about 30 mph (50 km/h). Winds blowing at up to double that speed are called gales. The strongest winds are hurricanes, the term used for winds blowing at over 75 mph (120 km/h). Meteorologists usually describe the force of the wind on the Beaufort scale, using figures from Force 0 (Calm air) to Force 12 (Hurricane force). The full scale appears in the Glossary.

Meteorologists measure the speed of the wind with an instrument called an anemometer. The cup anemometer illustrated is a common type.

We measure the direction of the wind with a wind vane. The rooster weather vane often seen on church steeples and other buildings is one kind of weather vane. It rotates freely and points in the direction in which the wind is blowing.

▲ This weather instrument is a cup anemometer. It measures the speed of the wind. The cups spin when the wind blows, and the rate at which they spin is a measure of the wind speed. Anemometers are often mounted with a wind vane, which measures wind direction.

Winds around the world

We saw earlier how differences in temperature between land and sea give rise to sea and land breezes. These breezes are very localized. But a similar process can occur on a much larger scale, involving whole continents. This happens in Asia, for example, notably in India, giving rise to winds that blow from sea to land during some months and from land to sea during others. Such winds are known as monsoons. (The word monsoon is Arabic for season.)

During the spring and early summer in India, the temperature of the land gradually rises. In June, the land becomes much hotter than the sea. This triggers off a wind that blows in over the land from the sea. This is the summer monsoon. Because it has come from over the sea, the wind is full of moisture, which it deposits over the land as torrential rain. As much as 30 feet (9 meters) of rain can fall in a month.

During fall and winter, the land cools down until it is much colder than the sea. This temperature difference now triggers the winter monsoon wind, which blows off the

22

IT'S AMAZING!

"Tubes" of wind, speeding at 100 mph (160 km/h) or more, blow around the world at heights of about 30,000-40,000 feet (9-12 km). They are called jet streams. They are thousands of miles long and usually blow from west to east. Airliners traveling from North America to Europe can reduce their flight time by an hour or more if they can "ride" the fast jet stream that blows over the North Atlantic.

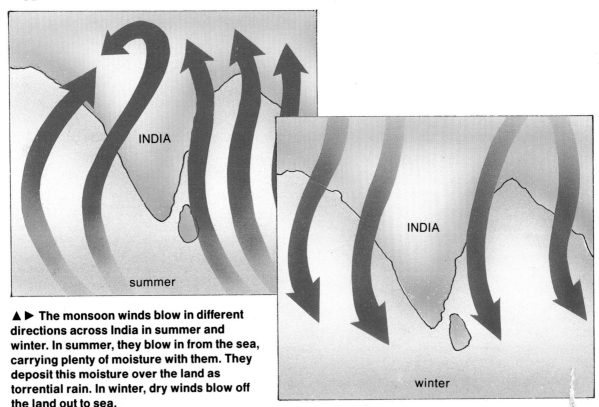

INDIA

summer

INDIA

winter

▲ ▶ The monsoon winds blow in different directions across India in summer and winter. In summer, they blow in from the sea, carrying plenty of moisture with them. They deposit this moisture over the land as torrential rain. In winter, dry winds blow off the land out to sea.

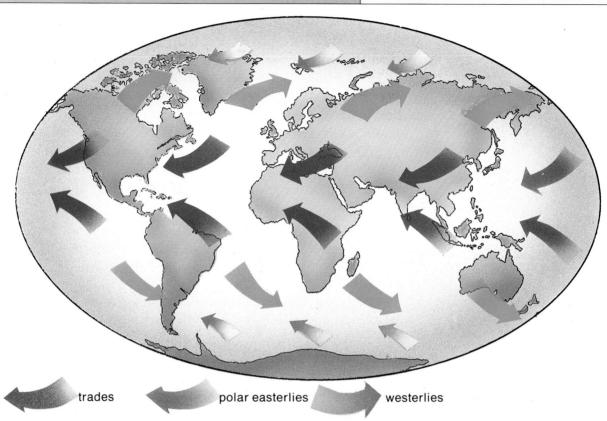

trades   polar easterlies   westerlies

land toward the sea. It is a dry wind, which dries up the land. If the summer monsoon is late in coming or for some reason fails to arrive, the land can become so parched that the crops fail and the population becomes desperately short of food.

Global wind belts

Temperature differences also occur at different latitudes on Earth because different latitudes receive different amounts of heat from the Sun. These temperature differences set up a pattern of winds that blow in much the same direction all the time. We call them prevailing winds.

The map above shows the main prevailing winds. Note that they travel in a diagonal direction. This happens because the Earth is rotating. The region on the Equator called the doldrums is an area of rapidly rising air. Its weather is notoriously unpredictable. Days of complete calm may follow periods of violent thunderstorms with torrential rainfall.

Q Why is the air in the doldrums rising rapidly?

▲ This map shows the main wind belts that exist around the world. The arrows show the direction in which the winds usually blow in different latitudes. In the days of sailing ships, sailors depended heavily on the so-called trade winds to speed their voyages around the world.

24

Stormy winds

Technically, a wind becomes a hurricane when it reaches a speed of 75 mph (120 km/h). But in the great tropical storms we call hurricanes, wind speeds have been known to reach 200 mph (320 km/h).

The characteristic feature of hurricanes is their spiral form. They are regions of violent winds rotating at high speed. They carry with them dense rain clouds that deposit torrential rain in their wake. Strangely, there is in the center of a hurricane an area of calm, which is called the eye. It averages about 20 miles (32 km) across. The hurricane itself can measure 350 miles (560 km) or more in diameter.

A typical hurricane that hits the United States is born as a storm in the middle of the Atlantic over hot tropical waters. It intensifies and develops its spiral form as it travels. Similar violent tropical storms spring up in the Pacific and Indian Oceans, where they are called cyclones or typhoons.

▼ This is what a hurricane looks like from space. The whirling winds make the clouds form a spiral pattern. They are heavy with moisture, which they unload as torrential rain.

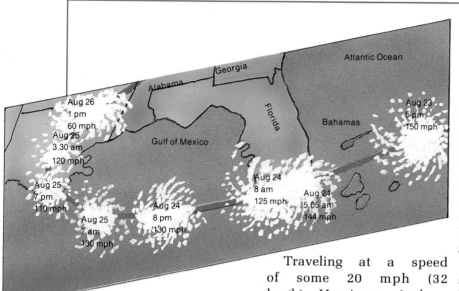

Hurricane Andrew

On August 24, 1992, the third most powerful hurricane to hit the United States this century smashed into southern Florida from the Atlantic.

Traveling at a speed of some 20 mph (32 km/h), Hurricane Andrew carved a swathe of devastation through Dade County, laying waste an area as big as the city of Chicago. Tens of thousands of homes were completely destroyed, and more than 150,000 people were left homeless. It was a miracle that there were only 65 deaths. Had Andrew struck areas of denser population farther north – Miami or Fort Lauderdale, for instance – the death toll would have been much greater.

When the hurricane struck, its winds were howling at speeds up to 150 mph (240 km/h), with gusts approaching 200 mph (320 km/h). The worst devastation occurred across a 25-mile (40-km) front, the region in which the winds were strongest.

Whirling winds

The winds in hurricanes reach amazing speeds, but the fastest winds of all occur in tornadoes. Many areas of the United States are prone to tornadoes – up to 500 can occur in the country every year. Where they hit, they are as devastating as a hurricane, although they do not affect such a large area. On the average, a tornado measures only about 300 feet (90 meters) across.

A tornado is a kind of funnel formed by rotating winds. Typically, it forms at the bottom of a thundercloud and corkscrews its way down to the ground. The winds in the tornado may reach speeds as high as 300 mph (500 km/h). Inside the "funnel" the air pressure is very low. So when the tornado hits a house, the air inside the house expands explosively, tearing it to pieces.

▶ **Tornadoes, popularly called "twisters," affect a much smaller area than hurricanes. But where they hit, they can cause just as much devastation.**

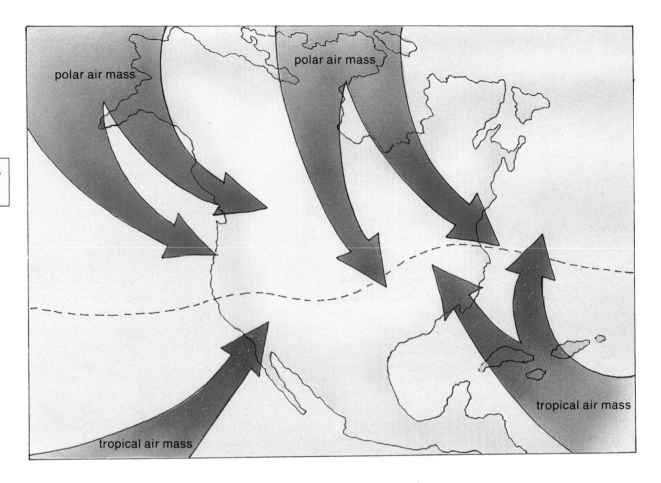

polar air mass

polar air mass

tropical air mass

tropical air mass

Air masses

Great masses of air with much the same temperature and moisture content wander across the globe. Meteorologists call them air masses. Much of our weather occurs when different air masses do battle.

The two main types of air masses around the world are the tropical air masses, born in the warm tropics, and the polar air masses, born over the polar regions. In the Northern Hemisphere, the warm tropical air masses travel north from the Equator to meet the cold polar air masses traveling south.

Weather fronts

The warm tropical and cold polar air masses meet at a boundary called the polar front. Collisions of these air masses on the northern polar front determine the weather

▲ During the winter over North America, cold air masses headed south from the Arctic do battle with warm air masses headed north from the tropics. They meet at a polar front, along which the weather is very unsettled.

▶ A cold front occurs when a wedge of cold air advances underneath a mass of warm air. The warm air is forced to rise, which cools it and causes clouds to form. Note in the diagram the saw-tooth symbol. This is used to denote a cold front on weather maps.

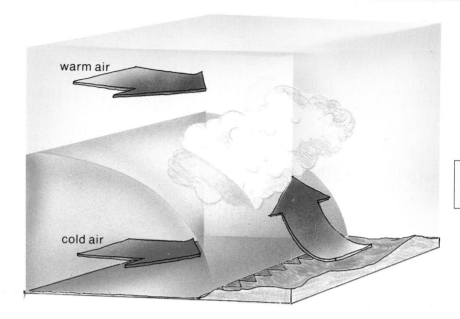

of a large part of the United States. They are also responsible for the stormy weather in the North Atlantic.

The diagrams show what happens when cold and warm air masses meet one another. Clouds form and often rain falls at the boundary between the two, creating a cold or a warm front. Often when tropical air masses and polar air masses struggle with one another on the polar front, the air begins to circle counterclockwise, with a warm front leading and a cold front coming up behind.

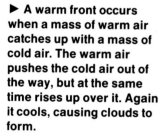

▶ A warm front occurs when a mass of warm air catches up with a mass of cold air. The warm air pushes the cold air out of the way, but at the same time rises up over it. Again it cools, causing clouds to form.

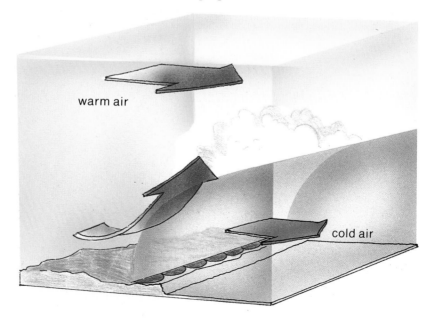

2
Moisture in the Air

◄ **Icicles and snow clothe a rocky mountainside. About one percent of the water in our world is snow and ice. Some of it circulates around the water cycle when the snow and ice melt. But much of it is locked in glaciers and the great ice sheets that cover the polar regions.**

Q Ice can break up rocks. How?

The Earth is a very watery planet – more than 70 percent of its surface is covered with water in one form or another. There is also water in the atmosphere, in the form of water gas, or vapor. The vapor enters the atmosphere when water evaporates from the surface. Water vapor is present only in minute quantities – it makes up less than one-thousandth of one percent of the air. But its presence has a marked effect on the weather. Under the right conditions, water vapor changes back into water droplets in the air, forming fog and clouds. This water eventually returns to the surface as rain, snow, hail, or dew.

The circulation of water from the surface into the atmosphere and back again is never-ending. We call it the water cycle. It is one of the most important of all natural processes.

► **Clouds bubble up over islands at sea, as here in the Hawaiian islands. Winds carrying moisture-laden air are forced to rise as they pass over the land. The air cools as it rises. Its moisture condenses into droplets, forming clouds.**

The water cycle

Every day about 30,500 cubic miles (125,000 cubic km) of water "disappear" from the oceans. This happens because the water evaporates, or turns to invisible vapor and mixes with the air. The oceans do not suffer a permanent loss of water, however, because a roughly equal amount of water is returned to them over the same period as part of the never-ending hydrologic, or water, cycle.

The oceans are the source of most, but by no means all, of the water vapor that enters the atmosphere. Water also evaporates from rivers and lakes, from the soil, and from vegetation.

Plants draw up water from the soil into their leaves to take part in their food-making process. But they take in much more water than they need and give off the excess as vapor through pores in the leaves. This process is known as transpiration.

▼ Two main processes are at work in the never-ending water cycle. One is evaporation, the other is condensation. Water evaporates from the surface and enters the air as water vapor. As it rises, the vapor condenses into water droplets, which form clouds. The water returns to the surface when it rains or snows.

Q 1. What causes the water to evaporate from the surface?

Q 2. What is a plant's food-making process called?

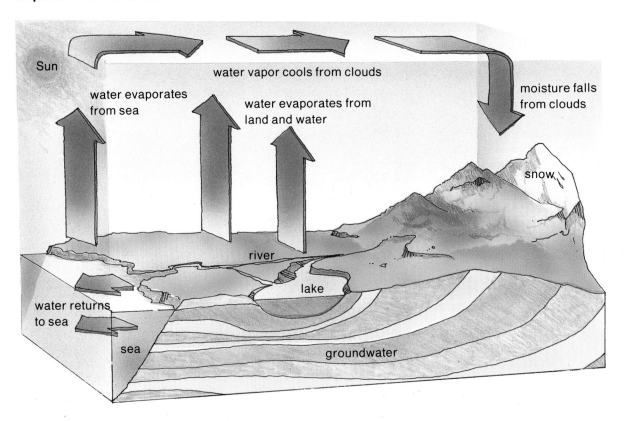

Sun

water vapor cools from clouds

water evaporates from sea

water evaporates from land and water

moisture falls from clouds

snow

river

lake

water returns to sea

sea

groundwater

▶ The dark color of the cloud in the distance warns that it is a rain cloud. And, sure enough, rain can be seen falling from it. It is only a local shower, however, covering a small area.

WORKOUT

The amount of water on the Earth's surface is about 1.4 trillion tons (1.3 trillion tonnes). Every year one-three-thousandth of this water evaporates into the air. Figure out how much water evaporates from the surface every day.

Vapor into water

Water vapor evaporated from the surface rises into the atmosphere. As it rises higher and higher, it cools because the temperature of the atmosphere falls with increasing height. Eventually the vapor is cold enough to condense, or turn back into liquid water. Condensation occurs around the microscopic dust particles that are nearly always present in the air. The fine water droplets that form gather together to make clouds.

Within the clouds, the tiny droplets jostle one another and join together to form larger drops. Eventually, the drops may become heavy enough to fall from the clouds. If the temperature is high enough, they fall as drops of rain. If the temperature is low enough, the moisture may freeze into tiny ice crystals which collect together to form snowflakes. Rain and snow are the most common forms of precipitation.

The rain or snow falls to the Earth's surface. In time, the rain water or melted snow find their way into the rivers, which flow into the oceans. The water cycle has now come full circle. Alternatively, the rain water may soak deep into the soil and remain there locked in the rocks for thousands of years.

Water vapor and humidity

As mentioned earlier, the amount of water vapor, or moisture, in the air plays a major role in determining the weather. This is because as the temperature changes the air may hold more or less moisture.

Warm air can hold more moisture than cold air: air at a temperature of 70°F (21°C) can hold twice as much moisture as air at 50°F (10°C).

At any temperature, when air has absorbed as much moisture as it can, it is said to be saturated. When saturated air is cooled, it can no longer hold as much moisture. So some of the moisture condenses – comes out of the air as liquid water. The temperature at which this happens is called the dew point.

The dew that forms on the grass on cold nights is one way in which the moisture comes out of the air. It forms when moist air near the ground is cooled and deposits its moisture in the form of glistening dewdrops. Light mists and denser fogs form when larger bodies of moist air cool and condense into tiny droplets around microscopic particles in the air.

▲ Dew drops on a seed head, turning into a dazzling jewel. Dew forms best on still clear nights, when the ground cools most.

32

INVESTIGATE

You can measure the humidity quite accurately by means of a wet-and-dry bulb hygrometer. See how it works in this experiment.

Take two ordinary room thermometers. Leave one as it is, but wrap some thick wool loosely around the bulb of the other one. Dip the end of the wool into water. Stand the thermometers side by side in the shade.

Record the thermometer readings from time to time. What did you notice about them? Compare the readings you take on a dry day with those you take on a humid day.

A similar process happens higher up in the atmosphere, when moist air rises and cools. The result is clouds.

It's the humidity

We call the amount of moisture in the air humidity. Humidity affects not only the weather, but also how we feel. On a hot day when the humidity is high, we feel "sticky" and uncomfortable. The heat makes our bodies perspire. But the perspiration cannot evaporate readily into the humid, moisture-laden air.

Humidity is usually expressed as a percentage. It is actually a relative humidity – being the amount of moisture in the air compared with the amount that would saturate the air. It is measured by instruments called hygrometers, such as the wet-and-dry-bulb type featured in the Investigation.

33

▼ **Early morning mists like this often form in the fall. But they soon disappear as the Sun rises and evaporates the mist droplets.**

Cirrus
These are the highest-level
clouds, popularly called mares'
tails.

34

Clouds

Clouds form when moisture-laden air rises into the atmosphere and cools. They may form at different levels in the atmosphere. At low levels — up to an altitude of about 6,500 feet (2,000 meters) — some of the water vapor in the air condenses into tiny droplets of liquid water, and it is billions of these droplets that form the cloud.

At high levels in the atmosphere — from about 20,000 feet (6,000 meters) upward — the air temperature is so low that the water vapor condenses into ice particles.

Cumulonimbus
These towering thunderclouds
are up to 5 miles (8 km) deep.
They are flat on the top and
bottom and are often shaped like
a blacksmith's anvil.

Classifying the clouds

Meteorologists classify clouds by their appearance and also by their height. The main kinds of clouds are cirrus, cumulus, stratus, and nimbus.

Cirrus are wispy, feathery-looking clouds that form high up and are made up entirely of ice crystals. Cumulus clouds are heaped-up white masses looking something like the head of a cauliflower. They are made up mainly of water droplets, but large ones may have ice crystals in their upper regions. Stratus clouds are somewhat featureless grey layers made up of water drops. Nimbus clouds are dark and shapeless and are heavy with rain.

The prefix "alto-" before one of the cloud forms indicates that it is a medium-level cloud. The prefix "cirro-" indicates that it is a high-level cloud.

Cirrocumulus
These high clouds form a large rippling formation that looks somewhat like the pattern on the body of a mackerel. The formation is often called a "mackerel sky."

Altostratus
This medium-level cloud formation takes the form of thick layers, through which the Sun can just be seen.

Cumulus
Fluffy white cumulus clouds are the typical clouds of summer. They bubble up as warm air rises from the hot ground and condenses.

Nimbostratus
This is the typical dark rain cloud ("nimbus" means rain). It often forms a thick layer all across the sky and brings heavy rain.

Rain and rainbows

Rain is the most common form of precipitation, or deposit of water, that falls from the sky. The water drops that make up rain can be up to about a quarter of an inch (5 mm) across during a thunderstorm, but usually they are much smaller.

Rain falls out of clouds. It forms in two main ways. In some rain clouds, air currents swirl around the tiny droplets of water that make up the cloud. As the droplets bump into one another, they join together, or coalesce. When they are big and heavy enough, they fall from the cloud as rain.

In clouds made up of ice crystals as well as water droplets, rain forms in another way. Air currents again swirl around the droplets and ice crystals. And water in the droplets freezes as soon as it touches the crystals. The crystals grow until they are heavy enough to fall from the cloud. If the air they fall through is warm, they melt to form raindrops.

Colors of the rainbow

When the Sun is low in the sky on rainy days, rainbows

36

WET WAI-'ALE-'ALE

The Hawaiian Islands are among the world's most popular vacation destinations. But visitors are advised to avoid Mt. Wai-'ale-'ale on the island of Kauai. The mountain has over 350 rainy days each year, and the total annual rainfall there exceeds 36 feet (11 meters). It is one of the wettest places on Earth.

Key to map

inches	mm.
over 120	over 3000
80-120	2000-3000
40-80	1000-2000
20-40	500-1000
10-20	250-500
under 10	under 250

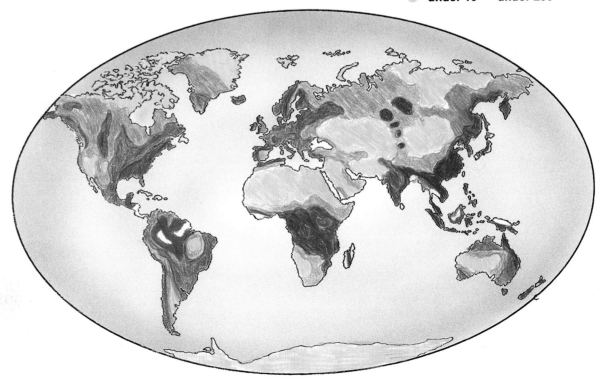

IT'S AMAZING!

A common expression referring to rain is "It's raining cats and dogs," meaning it's raining heavily. There is no reliable evidence to suggest that cats and dogs have rained down during a storm. But frogs and fish have been known to fall during rainstorms on occasions. They were probably carried aloft in the first place by whirlwinds or waterspouts.

◄◄ This map shows the average annual rainfall across the world. Note that the highest rainfall occurs in the tropics, where it rains on most days of the year. Little, if any, rain falls in the desert regions. In the Atacama Desert in Chile, to the west of the high Andes Mountains, it hasn't rained for centuries!

▶ A beautiful double rainbow. The inner and brighter of the two arcs is called the primary rainbow; the outer arc is called the secondary rainbow.

Q 3. What do you notice about the secondary arc, apart from its faintness?

often appear. They are beautiful bands of color that arch across the sky. From the inside of the arch to the outside, the main colors you see are violet, indigo, blue, green, yellow, orange, and red.

Q 1. Make up a mnemonic, or memory game, to help you remember the colors of the rainbow.

Light refraction

Rainbows form when raindrops split up sunlight into its different colors. (Sunlight is a mixture of many colors, or wavelengths, that blend together to make white light.)

The colors form when light is refracted (bent) by the curved surface of the raindrops. The raindrops act in much the same way as a glass prism.

Q 2. What is the name of the band of color formed when sunlight passes through a prism?

38

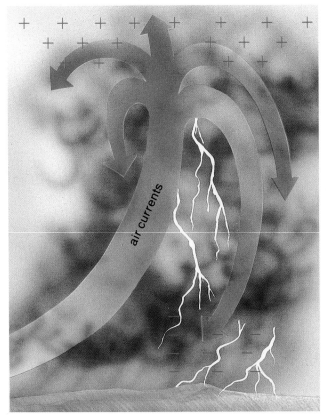

air currents

▲ An illustration of the probable process that takes place in a thundercloud. Powerful air currents swirl around the cloud particles, making them electrically charged. Particles with different charges settle in different parts of the cloud.

WORKOUT

You are having a thunderstorm, and you notice that you hear thunder 15 seconds after you see a lightning flash. Figure out how far away the thunderstorm is. The speed of sound in air near the ground is about 760 mph (1,200 km/h).

Thunder and lightning

Some of the heaviest rainfalls occur during thunderstorms. Thunderstorms are among the most spectacular phenomena in nature, bringing deafening thunderclaps and vivid flashes of lightning. The lightning strokes are discharges of electricity between clouds, or between clouds and the ground. They are in effect huge electric sparks.

Thunderstorms not only give rise to heavy rain, they also usually produce hail. Hail is a shower of icy balls called hailstones, which form when air currents carry icy particles up and down inside a thundercloud. As they travel, the particles pick up more water from droplets in the cloud. The water immediately freezes, and the droplets grow in this way until they are heavy enough to fall from the cloud. Hailstones can grow bigger than tennis balls and can cause severe damage when they reach the ground.

Inside the thundercloud

Thunderstorms, with their strong winds, heavy rain, hail, thunder, and lightning, are born in the gigantic clouds we call cumulonimbus. No one is certain exactly what happens in a thundercloud, but meteorologists feel that the following probably occurs.

Violent swirling air currents within the cloud cause the various particles within the cloud – ice particles, water droplets, and hailstones – to jostle one another. This causes friction, which gives the particles an electric charge. Light ice particles acquire a positive electric charge and gather near the top of the cloud. The heavier water droplets and hailstones acquire a negative charge and gather at the bottom of the cloud.

The buildup of positive and negative electric charges creates a very high voltage (electrical "pressure") between the charged areas, and between the cloud and the ground below. Voltages in the millions build up.

The voltage eventually becomes so high that the electricity discharges itself between the charged regions or down to the ground. We see this discharge as the elongated spark we call lightning. The air in the path of the lightning stroke is heated rapidly and expands explosively. This creates the noise we call thunder.

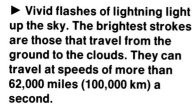

▶ Vivid flashes of lightning light up the sky. The brightest strokes are those that travel from the ground to the clouds. They can travel at speeds of more than 62,000 miles (100,000 km) a second.

Ⓠ 1. Is this speed slower or faster than the speed of light?

◀ The space shuttle Discovery thunders away from the launch pad. Its tall launch tower is protected from lightning strikes by an efficient lightning conductor. This is the white "pole" on top. The launch towers at Cape Canaveral are natural targets for lightning during thunderstorms.

Ⓠ 2. Why?

Frost and snow

On cool evenings, dew forms on plants and other objects when the air cools and its water vapor condenses (see page 30). If later the temperature falls below freezing, the liquid dew drops will freeze to form the icy coating we call frost.

If the temperature falls rapidly below freezing, the water vapor in the air condenses directly as ice crystals, without forming liquid water first. We often call this kind of frost hoar frost.

Q 1. Do you know the scientific name for the process in which a vapor changes directly to a solid without forming liquid first?

Snowflakes

Like rain, snow is born in the clouds. Indeed, some rain begins life as snow, which later melts when it falls from the clouds into warm air. But if the air beneath the clouds is below freezing, the snow remains frozen and falls to the ground.

Snow may fall throughout the year in the cold polar regions – in the Arctic and Antarctic. It may also fall at any time at the summit of high mountains, where the temperature is always below freezing. But over the temperate regions of the world, snow falls mostly in the winter. In tropical and subtropical regions, it almost never snows.

In North America, the high Rockies, Sierra Nevada, and Cascade mountain ranges in the west experience the highest snowfalls. The heaviest annual snowfall yet recorded in the world took place at Paradise, Mt. Rainier, the highest peak in the Cascades. Between February 1971 and February 1972, 102 feet (31 meters) of snow fell.

▲ Feathery patterns of ice appear on a window pane after a frosty night. In folklore they are said to be the handiwork of an imaginary character.

Q 2. What is he called?

▶ A snow scene in the Appalachians, the main mountain range in eastern North America.

▲ A snowflake photographed under a microscope. This exquisite icy jewel resembles all other snowflakes in that it has a basic six-pointed star shape. But its intricate design differs in detail from that of every other snowflake. Each snowflake is unique.

INVESTIGATE

If you live in a part of the country that has cold winters, measure the depth of snow that falls. All you need is an ordinary ruler. Make sure you use snow that has not been walked on. By melting some snow in a saucepan, find out how much snow is equivalent to one inch (25 mm) of rainfall.

3 Seasons and Climate

◀ **Death Valley, in California, is one of the hottest places on Earth. Here the temperature frequently soars to more than 120°F (49°C) in summer. Rainfall throughout the year is minimal. Little plant life can grow under such harsh conditions.**

Q **Death Valley is notable not only for its high temperatures, but for another reason. What is it?**

▶ **In Hawaii, plants grow in profusion because of the hot, moist tropical climate. This royal poinciana tree thrives under such conditions, displaying an abundance of spectacular blooms. Alternative names for it are flamboyant tree and flame tree.**

In regions around the Equator, the weather stays much the same all the time – it is hot and it rains a lot. But in many parts of the world, a gradual change in the weather occurs throughout the year. This is true for much of North America and Europe, for example.

We call these regular changes in the weather the seasons. Regions of the world on either side of the Equator experience just two seasons – one hot and wet, and the other hot and dry. Regions farther away from the Equator experience four seasons – spring, summer, fall, and winter.

In any particular region, the weather usually changes from day to day and from season to season. But year after year, the weather pattern remains much the same. We call these typical regional weather patterns the climate. All kinds of different climates – from very hot to very cold, and from very wet to very dry – can be found in different parts of the world.

◄ Spring in the Northern Hemisphere begins on March 21. This is the time of the year when the effects of the Sun are gaining strength, stirring nature to life after the cold of winter. Buds burst into leaf, flowers start to bloom, animals mate and raise their young.

► Summer in the Northern Hemisphere begins on June 21. This is the hottest time of the year, when the Sun climbs highest in the sky and the hours of daylight are longest. Nature is in full bloom. Crops are growing in the fields, awaiting the harvest.

◄ Fall, or autumn, in the Northern Hemisphere begins on September 23. This time of the year is marked by falling leaves and falling temperatures. Animals such as squirrels gather food for the coming winter. Many species of birds and other animals migrate south to escape the cold.

► Winter in the Northern Hemisphere begins on December 21. This is the coldest time of the year, when the Sun is at its lowest in the sky and the hours of daylight are shortest. Many plants die after seeding; others remain dormant ("sleeping"), waiting for the warmth of spring to stir them to life. Many animals become dormant, too. They hibernate, or sleep, through the winter.

44

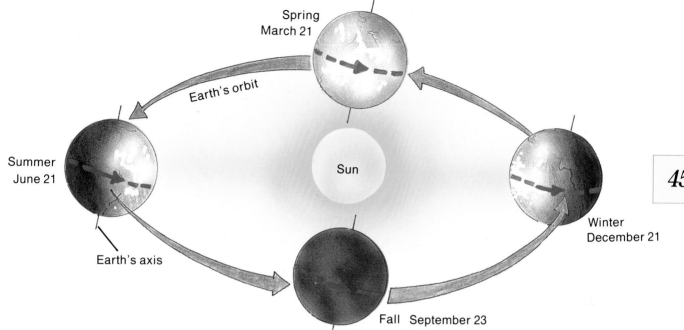

Spring
March 21

Earth's orbit

Summer
June 21

Sun

Earth's axis

Winter
December 21

Fall   September 23

▲ The positions of the Earth in relation to the Sun at four significant times of the year. On June 21, the Northern Hemisphere is tilted most toward the Sun, and it is summer. On December 21, the Northern Hemisphere is tilted most away from the Sun, and it is winter. On March 21, the axis is "side on" to the Sun, being tilted neither toward nor away from it. On this date, the length of the day and the night are equal. It is called the spring equinox ("equal night"). On September 23, the Earth's axis is again "side on" to the Sun, and day and night are again of equal length. It is the autumnal equinox.

The four seasons

Many parts of the world, including the United States, experience a noticeable change in the weather throughout the year. It is marked by the four seasons of spring, summer, fall, and winter.

The main feature of the weather that changes with the seasons is the temperature. The weather becomes warmer from winter through spring to summer, then gets colder from summer through fall (autumn) back to winter.

The tilted axis

The diagram above helps explain why the seasonal changes in temperature occur. They occur because of the way the Earth spins as it travels in space in its orbit around the Sun.

The axis on which the Earth spins is tilted at an angle to the plane of its path around the Sun. The axis points in the same direction in space all the time. This means that as the Earth circles the Sun during the year, a particular region is tilted more toward the Sun at some times than at others. When it is tilted more toward the Sun, it receives more heat and experiences higher temperatures.

Q   What would happen to the seasons if the Earth's axis were not tilted?

Climates of the world

Different parts of the world experience different patterns of weather throughout the year – they are said to have different climates.

The two main features that affect a climate are the temperature and the rainfall. Both greatly influence the average weather pattern and also determine the kind of vegetation that grows. This in turn determines what animal species inhabit the region.

Changing temperatures

Temperature is by far the most important aspect of climate. The temperature of a region depends largely on the amount of heat it receives from the Sun. This depends in turn on where the region is located on Earth. Because the Earth's surface is curved, some parts receive more heat

46

▼ Major climatic regions of the world. Regions around the North and South Poles and on high mountains have the coldest climates. Regions within the tropics, on either side of the Equator, have the hottest climates. Note the vast areas of the world that have a dry climate.

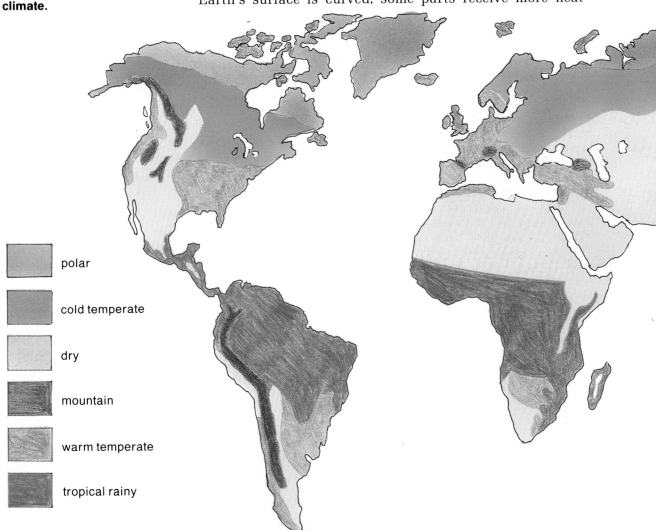

polar

cold temperate

dry

mountain

warm temperate

tropical rainy

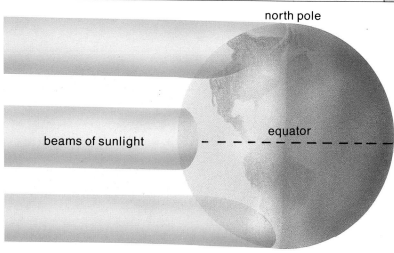

north pole

beams of sunlight

equator

south pole

▶ Imagine three beams of sunlight of equal size falling on the Earth at the Poles and at the Equator. At the Equator, the beam is spread over the least area. At the Poles, it is spread over the most. This is why regions near the Equator are hotter than those near the Poles.

Q Here we show the beam of sunlight falling vertically onto the Earth's surface at the Equator. On what date does this happen?

than others. This can be seen from the diagram above.

The equatorial regions – around the Equator – receive the most solar heat and are hottest. The polar regions – around the North and South Poles – receive the least solar heat and are coldest. Between these two extremes are the temperate regions, which have a more moderate climate, being neither very cold nor very hot.

The diagram above also explains why the temperature of a region changes with the seasons. As the axis of the Earth tilts with respect to the Sun, a region receives more or less solar heat.

The tropics

The Sun is located directly over the Equator twice a year, on the equinoxes. On March 21, it passes over the Equator as it appears to travel north. On June 21, it reaches its most northerly position relative to the Equator. It is then directly over latitude 23½° north. This latitude line is called the Tropic of Cancer.

The Sun then begins traveling south. And on September 23, it is again over the Equator. On December 21, it reaches its most southerly position relative to the Equator. It is then directly over latitude 23½° south. This latitude line is called the Tropic of Capricorn.

The region between the two Tropic lines is called the tropics. The climate within this region is often referred to as tropical. The climate of regions just to the north and south of the tropics is called subtropical.

◄ Lush vegetation covers the beautiful tropical islands of Bali, Indonesia, in Southeast Asia. The island is located a few degrees south of the equator, and experiences constant warmth and plentiful rainfall. Palms, rice, and bananas grow well under these conditions.

▼ Tree frogs like this thrive in hot, moist climates and are found widely in tropical and subtropical regions.

Hot climates

Regions on and near the Equator enjoy the hottest and also the wettest climate on Earth. The temperature averages about 77°F (25°C) all year round. Rain falls almost every day, and there is up to 13 ft (4 meters) of rainfall in places.

In such a constantly hot and moist climate, plant life flourishes in abundance. Trees and other vegetation grow quickly, and many flower and fruit continuously. The typical tree has broad leaves and is evergreen. Mahogany and teak are among important species, yielding valuable hardwood.

In South America, Africa, and Asia, dense rain forests grow in the equatorial regions. Their uppermost branches form a continuous layer called the canopy, which can extend over areas of hundreds of square miles. Beneath the canopy there are lower layers of shorter trees and shrubs. The forest floor is dark because little sunlight can filter through the dense vegetation. The forest floor and the various layers above it form different habitats for a rich variety of animals, from elephants and leopards in the undergrowth to monkeys and parrots in the canopy.

The savanna

North and south of the African rain forests there are vast regions of tropical grassland, called the savanna. Similar regions in South America are called the llanos. Unlike the rain forests, these grasslands do not have the same climate all year round. They have two distinct seasons – wet and dry. No rain falls at all during the dry season, which is up to six months long.

Like the rain forests, the savanna teems with wildlife, particularly grazing animals such as antelope and zebra. These animals in turn provide food for the meat-eating hunters such as lion and cheetah.

Q **1.** What is the correct name for a plant-eating animal? A meat-eating animal?

▼ **(Below) Rippling sand dunes in the Sahara Desert. The relentless Sun and the lack of appreciable rainfall make this desert one of the most inhospitable places on the face of the Earth. It is the largest of the world's deserts, occupying some 3,000,000 square miles (nearly 8 million sq km).**

Q **2. Is this area bigger than or smaller than the area of the United States?**

▼ **(Bottom) The scorpion is a creature of the desert, where it feeds mainly on insects and spiders. It kills with the poisonous stinger it has at the tip of its curved tail.**

Q **3. To which creatures are scorpions most closely related, insects or spiders?**

50

Temperate climates

Much of the warm temperate regions of the world are taken up by grasslands. In North America, they are known as the prairie; in South America, the pampas; and in Asia, the steppes.

It is on these grasslands that farmers cultivate cereal grasses, such as wheat, on a vast scale and graze livestock by the million. To a large extent, these farmed species have replaced the natural wildlife, such as buffalo and deer.

Productive farmland is also found throughout the rest of the warm temperate regions, which were once heavily forested. Today, little natural forest land remains. The typical trees of the region are hardwoods such as the beech, elm, oak, and ash. These species are deciduous, which means they shed their leaves in the fall.

▲ Grapes thrive in warm, temperate climates that have a moist and not very cold winter and a hot, dry summer. This type of climate is known as Mediterranean, for it is typical of the lands around the Mediterranean Sea in Europe.

▶ Picking grapes in Bulgaria, much of which enjoys a Mediterranean climate. California enjoys a similar climate, which is one reason its wines are so good.

Q What is the name of the process that turns grape juice into wine?

The boreal forests

The cold temperate regions of the world are occupied largely by dense forests. These forests are found in the north of North America, Europe, and Asia. They are often called the "boreal" forests. The name comes from "Boreus," the name the ancient Greeks gave to their god of the north wind.

In the boreal forests, the typical tree is the evergreen conifer, such as fir, pine, and spruce. These trees are well adapted to the climate, with its short summers and long, cold, and snowy winters. They have narrow leaves like needles, which do not lose moisture as readily as broad leaves.

Q Most species of conifers are cone-shaped, narrow at the top and broad at the base. What advantage do you think this shape gives them?

▼ **Fall in a beechwood. The beech is a typical tree of temperate climates. It is a broad-leafed hardwood tree, which is deciduous.**

▼ **The Red fox is found widely in deciduous woods throughout the temperate U.S. and Europe. It can also live in both hotter and colder climates.**

51

Polar bears and penguins live in cold polar regions. With its thick fur and a layer of fat under its skin, the polar bear is well adapted to living in freezing temperatures. The penguin spends a lot of time in the water, which in polar climates is warmer than the air.

Q Polar bears are great hunters. They would hunt and kill penguins if they could. Why can't they?

Cold climates

The coldest climates on Earth are found in the extreme north and south of our world, in the Arctic, close to the North Pole; and in the Antarctic, close to the South Pole. These regions have what is called a polar climate, in which winter temperatures can plummet to $-60°F$ ($-50°C$) and below. The ground is permanently covered by snow and ice. Nothing can grow there.

In the Arctic, sandwiched between the boreal forest belt and the permanent snows, is a desolate region called the tundra. It experiences very harsh winters, but is warm enough in the brief summer to allow some hardy plants and shrubs to grow. There is no tundra region in the Antarctic.

As the snows melt, the explosion of growth on the Artic tundra attracts many species of birds to breed, particularly geese. Larger animals, such as caribou, also flock there from the forests. Both birds and caribou migrate south before the winter cold returns.

Mountain climates

You would not expect to find permanent snow and ice near the Equator, would you? But in fact you do – in Africa. You find snow and ice on Africa's two highest mountain peaks, Mt. Kenya (17,058 ft, 5,200 meters) and Mt. Kilimanjaro (19,340 ft, 5,895 meters), which are only a few degrees south of the Equator.

Mountains have a different kind of climate from the land that surrounds them. This is because the temperature falls as you climb higher.

If you climbed Kilimanjaro, you would experience a whole range of climates in which particular vegetation thrived. You would climb from the hot surrounding savanna through warm rain forest, cool swampland, and a bleak, tundra-like landscape, into a region of permanent snow. The snow line occurs at an altitude of about 15,000 feet (4,600 meters). There the temperature is always below freezing.

53

▼ As you climb the slopes of Mt. Kilimanjaro, you pass through layers of vegetation typical of different kinds of climates, from tropical savanna at the lowest level to a polar region at the highest.

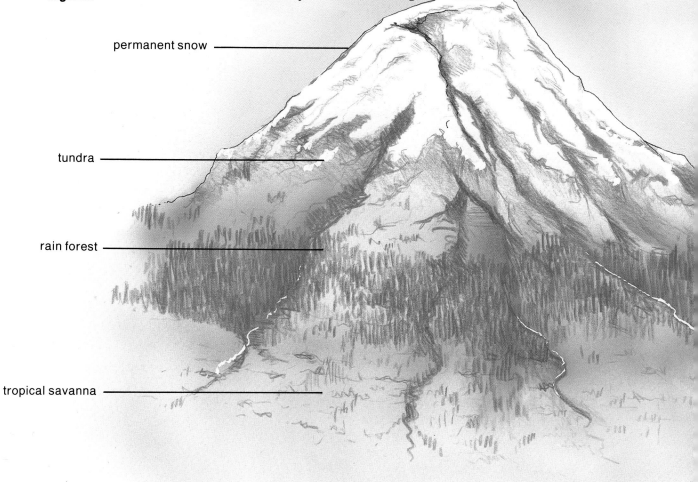

permanent snow

tundra

rain forest

tropical savanna

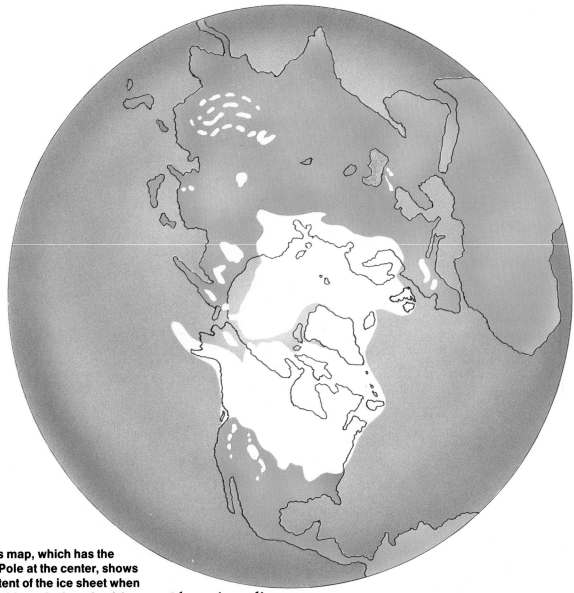

▲ This map, which has the North Pole at the center, shows the extent of the ice sheet when the world was in the grip of the last great ice age, some 30,000 years ago. In North America, glaciers extended as far south as Kansas City, Missouri.

Changing climates

On average, the climate of a region does not change markedly from year to year. But over longer periods, it can change dramatically.

Only 30,000 years ago – a mere moment in geological time – vast ice sheets covered much of North America, northern Europe, and Asia when the world was experiencing one of its periodic ice ages.

Ice ages occur when the Earth cools down. The average temperature of the world needs to drop only a few degrees for this to happen.

The drop in world temperatures occurs from time to time mainly because changes in the Earth's orbit reduce the amount of heat it receives from the Sun. Later, as the Earth's orbit continues to change, the Sun begins to pour more heat onto the Earth and the ice sheets retreat.

The periods between the ice ages are known as interglacials (literally, "between the glaciers"). We are in an interglacial period at present. One day, the glaciers could return and bring another ice age to the Earth.

Temporary cooling of the climate can occur over much shorter periods. This happens when volcanoes erupt and eject huge masses of ash into the air. Much of this ash falls back to the ground quickly, but large amounts get into the stratosphere and stay there for months or even years. Up in the stratosphere, they block the Sun's rays and reduce the amount of heat reaching the ground.

Warming up

Human activities also appear to be bringing about changes in the climate. Burning fuels in motor vehicles and power stations releases huge amounts of carbon dioxide into the air. This heavy gas increases the greenhouse effect, which is slowly causing world temperatures to rise.

▶ **Natural and man-made influences that pollute the air and affect the climate. Volcanic eruptions throw out vast amounts of ash and fumes. Clearing the forests by burning releases carbon dioxide, a gas also given out in copious amounts by the engines of cars, trucks, trains, planes, and other means of transportation. Even cattle play their part by giving off methane, a greenhouse gas like carbon dioxide.**

55

Milestones

ABOUT 330 BC The Greek philosopher Aristotle wrote what is thought to be the first scientific study of the weather, "Meteorologica."

ABOUT 1500 The Italian artist and inventor Leonardo da Vinci made a detailed study of the weather and designed an improved weather vane.

1597 The Italian scientist Galileo developed the first practical thermometer.

1643 The Italian mathematician Evangelista Torricelli discovered the principle of the barometer.

1752 American scientist and statesman Benjamin Franklin in Philadelphia first carried out his famous kite experiment in a thunderstorm and developed the lightning rod (conductor) to protect buildings from lightning strikes.

1805 British naval officer Francis Beaufort devised the Beaufort wind force scale for estimating wind speed.

1815 The volcano Tambora in Indonesia erupted, sending so much ash into the air that it persisted in the atmosphere for years. In 1816, the ash in the atmosphere cooled the Earth so much that it was called the "year without a summer."

1849 The Smithsonian Institution asked operators of the newly invented Morse telegraph to begin their transmissions each day with brief information on the weather. The information was then converted into a simple weather chart. Physicist Joseph Henry was one of the first to work on telegraphed weather reports.

1853 Representatives of major shipping nations met at Brussels, in Belgium, to discuss coordinating weather observations and reports from ships.

1878 Representatives of weather organizations around the world met at Utrecht, in the Netherlands, and set up the International Meteorological Organization.

1913 A temperature of 134°F (57°C) was recorded in Death Valley, California, the highest temperature recorded anywhere on Earth until that time.

1922 A temperature of 136.4°F (58°C) was recorded at Al'Aziziyah in Libya. No higher temperature has been recorded since.

1946 American researchers Vincent Schaefer and Irving Langmuir first demonstrated that clouds could be "seeded" with dry ice (solid carbon dioxide) to make them shed their moisture.

1951 The International Meteorological Organization changed its name to the World Meteorological Organization and became an agency of the United Nations. Its headquarters are now in Geneva, Switzerland.

1960 The United States launched the first weather satellite, Tiros 1. Its two television cameras sent back pictures of cloud cover over the Earth.

1971 Rain fell in the Atacama Desert in Chile, South America, for the first time in 400 years.

1983 A temperature of -128.6°F (-89.2°C) was recorded at Vostok in Antarctica. This is the lowest temperature ever recorded on Earth.

1992 The United States suffered the most destructive hurricane this century, Hurricane Andrew. It killed 65 people and caused damage estimated to be in the region of 30 billion dollars.

Glossary

AIR MASS A large mass of air with much the same temperature and moisture content throughout.

AIR PRESSURE See ATMOSPHERIC PRESSURE.

ANEMOMETER An instrument that measures the speed of the wind.

ANTICYCLONE A term for a region of high pressure.

ATMOSPHERE The layer of air that surrounds the Earth. More generally, a layer of gases that surrounds a heavenly body, such as a planet or a moon.

ATMOSPHERIC PRESSURE The pressure exerted by the atmosphere. At sea level, the atmospheric pressure is about 14.7 pounds per square inch (1 kg per square cm). The pressure decreases as you climb above sea level.

BAR The unit with which meteorologists measure atmospheric pressure. They usually quote pressures as so many millibars, or thousandths of a bar.

BAROMETER An instrument that measures the pressure of the atmosphere. A barograph is a barometer that records the pressure as an ink trace on paper.

BEAUFORT SCALE A scale for estimating wind force (speed) from its effect on the surroundings (see Box).

BREEZE A light wind.

CIRRUS A high-level cloud that has a wispy appearance.

CLIMATE The general pattern of weather over a long period of time.

CLOUD A mass of little water droplets or ice crystals in the sky.

COLD FRONT The boundary formed when a cold air mass pushes away a warm air mass.

CONDENSATION A process in which water vapor in the atmosphere changes back into water when it is cooled. It is the opposite of evaporation.

CONVECTION A process in which warm air rises in the atmosphere because it is lighter (less dense) than the surrounding cold air.

CUMULUS A cloud that somewhat resembles a pile of cotton.

CYCLONE This has two meanings in meteorology. One, a cyclone is a region of low pressure. Two, a tropical cyclone is an intense storm. Hurricanes and typhoons are examples of tropical cyclones.

DEPRESSION A region of low pressure.

DEW Water drops that appear on surfaces when the Earth cools down at night.

The Beaufort Scale

Wind force	Wind name	Wind speed mph	Wind speed km/h	Effects on surroundings
0	Calm air	0-1	0-1	Smoke rises vertically
1	Light air	2-3	2-5	Smoke is slightly bent
2	Light breeze	4-7	6-11	Leaves start to rustle
3	Gentle breeze	8-12	12-19	Leaves start to move
4	Moderate breeze	13-18	20-29	Small branches move
5	Fresh breeze	19-24	30-38	Small trees bend
6	Strong breeze	25-31	39-49	Large branches move
7	Moderate gale	32-38	50-60	Large trees bend
8	Fresh gale	39-46	61-74	Twigs start to break
9	Strong gale	47-54	75-86	Roofs suffer damage
10	Whole gale	55-63	87-100	Trees are uprooted
11	Storm	64-75	101-120	Damage is widespread
12	Hurricane	Over 75	Over 120	Severe destruction occurs

DEW POINT The temperature at which water vapor in the atmosphere begins to condense into liquid water.

DOLDRUMS A region around the Equator where the wind is often light or absent.

DRIZZLE A form of very light rain with small drops that fall from low clouds.

EQUINOXES Times of the year when the Sun lies directly over the Equator and when the hours of daylight and nighttime are equal all over the world. The spring, or vernal, equinox is on March 21, and the autumnal equinox is on September 23.

EVAPORATION The process in which liquid water changes into water vapor. It is the opposite of condensation.

FOG A "cloud" of fine water droplets suspended in the air at ground level.

FROST The icy coating on the ground that occurs when the temperature is below freezing. Water vapor freezes as it condenses from the air.

FRONT The boundary between two different air masses. See COLD FRONT, WARM FRONT.

GALE A strong wind.

GREENHOUSE EFFECT A process in which the atmosphere acts like a greenhouse and traps some of the heat from the Sun.

GROUNDWATER Water that is held in the soil and rocks.

HAIL A form of precipitation consisting of little balls of ice.

HIGH A region of high pressure; an anticyclone.

HUMIDITY The amount of moisture in the atmosphere, in the form of water vapor.

HURRICANE The name given to the destructive tropical cyclones that occur in the Caribbean Sea and the Gulf of Mexico.

HYGROMETER An instrument that measures the humidity of the air.

IONOSPHERE The layer of atmosphere above the stratosphere, where the gases in the air are present as ions, or electrically charged atoms.

ISOBAR A line on a weather map connecting places with the same atmospheric pressure.

JET STREAM A fast-moving current of air high in the atmosphere.

LIGHTNING The light given out when electricity "jumps" between clouds or between the clouds and the ground.

LOW A region of low pressure; also called a depression or cyclone.

METEOROLOGY The science of the atmosphere and weather.

MONSOON A seasonal wind that blows in different directions at different times of the year.

NIMBUS A rain cloud.

OZONE LAYER A region in the upper atmosphere that contains the gas ozone and filters out harmful rays from sunlight.

POLAR Around the North or the South Pole.

PRECIPITATION Liquid water that falls from the clouds as rain, snow, or hail.

PREVAILING WIND One that blows from the same general direction for most of the time.

RAIN The most common kind of precipitation.

SEASONS Periods of the year marked by characteristic changes in the weather.

SLEET Precipitation consisting of a mixture of rain and snow.

STORM A very strong wind.

STRATOSPHERE The layer of atmosphere above the troposphere.

STRATUS A low-level layer cloud.

SYNOPTIC CHART A weather map showing the state of the weather at a particular time, prepared during weather forecasting.

TEMPERATE REGIONS Part of the Earth's surface between the polar regions and the tropics.

THERMOMETER An instrument that measures temperature.

THUNDER The noise made when a lightning stroke heats the air in its path, which expands explosively.

TORNADO A very destructive wind storm, consisting of a rapidly spinning column of air.

TRANSPIRATION The process in which plants give off water vapor through their leaves.

TROPICS The region spanning the Equator between latitude 23½ degrees north (the Tropic of Cancer) and latitude 23½ degrees south (the Tropic of Capricorn).

TROPOSPHERE The lowest layer in the atmosphere, in which most of our weather takes place.

TUNDRA The barren landscape of the far north, in the Arctic.

TWISTER A popular name for a tornado.

TYPHOON The name given to tropical cyclones that take place in the Far East.

WARM FRONT The boundary formed when a warm air mass pushes away a cold air mass.

WATER CYCLE The never-ending interchange of water between the ground and the atmosphere.

WATER VAPOR Water in the form of a gas. Tiny amounts of water vapor in the atmosphere have a great influence on the weather.

WEATHER VANE An instrument that indicates the direction of the wind.

59

Answers

Page 8
A solar flame is a mass of gas heated so much that it glows. The heat comes from nuclear reactions taking place inside the Sun. A candle flame is the light produced when candle wax burns in air. The heat is produced as a result of a chemical reaction.

Page 11
The dark areas are the Great Lakes.

Page 15
1. The fastest winds on Saturn travel at speeds of over 1,090 mph (1,750 km/h).
2. Nitrogen is the main gas in the atmosphere of our own planet, Earth.
3. You could fit two Earths comfortably into Jupiter's Great Red Spot.

Page 17
The atmosphere at the Equator is hot, and hot air occupies a greater volume than cold air.

Page 18
Wood, coal, oil, gas, and other fuels give off carbon dioxide when they burn in air.

Investigation
In the experiment, the burning candle used up all the oxygen in the air, and the water rose in the jar to take its place. You can estimate roughly the proportion of oxygen in the air by measuring with a ruler the amount it rose in the jar compared with the depth of the jar. You should find that oxygen occupies about a fifth of the air. The exact figure is 21 percent.

Page 19
Workout
The weight of air pressing on your palm would be greater in New York City than in Denver. This is because New York is located at sea level, while Denver stands at an altitude of 1 mile (1.6 km). That's why it's called the Mile High City.
1. The ultraviolet rays that get through the ozone layer tan our skin, or burn it if we stay out in the sun too long.
2. In the simpler design, the end of the pointer would move only a little, making slight air pressure changes difficult to see. The pivot and lever mechanism attached to the bellows magnifies its movement, making the end of the pointer move a lot for a slight change in air pressure.

Page 23
The air in the doldrums rises rapidly because it is located above the part of the Earth that receives the most heat from the Sun.

Page 29
Water trickles into crevices in the rocks and on cold nights freezes into ice. As the water freezes, it expands (ice takes up more space than water). The forces produced by this expansion are great enough to split the rock.

Page 30
1. The heat from the Sun.
2. A plant's food-making process is called photosynthesis.

Page 31
Workout
Some 1.3 billion tons (1.2 billion tonnes) of water evaporate from the Earth's surface every day.

Page 32
Investigation
The thermometer readings are different – the wet bulb registers a lower temperature than the dry one. This is because water is evaporating from the wet one, and when water evaporates it takes in heat. The water evaporates faster when the air is dry

than when the air is wet, and so the wet bulb thermometer has a lower reading.

Page 37
1. A suitable mnemonic to help you remember the colors of the spectrum might be: "Very Irritating Boys and Girls Yell Outrageous Rhymes."
The first letter of each word reminds you of a color, and the rhyme includes the colors in their correct order in the arc of the spectrum.
2. The band of color formed when sunlight passes through a prism is called a spectrum. A rainbow is a spectrum formed in the sky.
3. In the secondary arc of a rainbow, the colors are reversed, with red on the inside of the arc and indigo on the outside.

Page 38
Workout
If you hear a clap of thunder 15 seconds after a lightning flash, the thundersorm is about 3 miles (5 km) away.

Page 39
1. A lightning stroke travels more slowly than the speed of light, which travels at a speed of 186,000 miles (300,000 km) a second. In any case, nothing can travel faster than the speed of light.
2. The landscape at Cape Canaveral is very flat, so the tops of the launch towers are the highest points around.

Page 40
1. The scientific name for the change in state from a vapor to a solid (or the other way around) is sublimation.
2. The imaginary character who is supposed to make icy patterns on windowpanes is Jack Frost.

Page 41
Investigation
Depending on how wet the snow is (some snow is wetter than others), it can take

between about 6 inches (15 cm) and 30 inches (75 cm) of snow to equal the water in 1 inch (2.5 cm) of rainfall.

Page 43
Death Valley is the lowest point in the United States and, indeed, in the Western Hemisphere. It is some 282 feet (86 meters) below sea level.

Page 45
If the Earth's axis were not tilted, there would be no seasons. Each latitude would receive the same amount of heat from the Sun all through the year.

Page 47
The Sun is directly over the Equator at the times of the equinoxes – on March 21 and on September 23 every year.

Page 49
1. A plant-eating animal is called a herbivore, and a meat-eating one is called a carnivore.
2. The Sahara Desert has an area slightly smaller than that of the United States (about 3,615,000 square miles or 9,362,000 square km).
3. Scorpions are closely related to spiders. They are both classed as arachnids.

Page 50
The process that turns grape juice into wine is called fermentation.

Page 51
The cone shape of a conifer tree helps prevent too much snow from accumulating on the branches. If snow piled up, it could break the branches if they were spread as in a deciduous tree.

Page 52
Fortunately for penguins, they live literally poles apart from polar bears. They are found only near the South Pole, while polar bears are found only near the North Pole.

For further reading

Branley, franklyn.
Flash, Crash, Rumble, and Roll.
Harper and Row, New York. 1985.

Fradin, Dennis.
Blizzards and Winter Weather.
Childrens Press, Chicago, IL. 1983.

Knapp, Brian.
Storm.
Raintree Steck-Vaughn, Austin, TX. 1989.

Knapp, Brian.
Weather.
Raintree Steck-Vaughn, Austin, TX. 1989.

Lambert, David.
Weather and its Work.
Facts on File, New York. 1984.

Leggett, Jeremy and Dennis Leggett.
Air Scare.
Marshall Cavendish, New York. 1991.

Lye, Kenneth.
Weather and Climate.
Silver Burdett, Morristown, NJ. 1984.

Williams, Terry.
The Secret Language of Snow.
Sierra Club Books, San Francisco, CA. 1984.

Index

Numbers in *italics* refer to illustrations.

63